Author's Note About Dogs and Wolves

I first started to summarize our communications research in a reportage style. To change the pace, I inserted, on a whim, a conversation with my dog, trying to explain why many of us are challenged by our interpersonal communications.

When I tested the results on a few select clients, all said: Scrap the journalistic approach, and present the material through the eyes of your dog!!

Hence this more fun approach, a dialogue through the voice of Calypso. It allowed him to challenge the material, and me to explain it all – in a different and more entertaining way.

We later added the image of the wolf on the front cover, as a symbol of the ultimate communicator.

If only we could all communicate as well as the wolf – and our pets!

MASTERING COMMUNICATIONS™
Copyright © 2008 by Roger HB Davies

All characters in this book are fictitious. Any resemblance to someone you know is entirely deliberate.

ISBN 0-9734356-0-7

10   9   8   7   6   5   4   3   2   1

Published by
Springboard Books, Inc.
15 Delisle Avenue
Toronto, Ontario, Canada
M4V 1S8

TEL   416.928.3131
FAX   416.928.1298
E-mail   mastering@mdctraining.ca
www.mdctraining.ca

Printed and bound in Canada

Springboard Books Inc.

Graphic Design	Line of Sight Design Associates Inc.
Illustrations	Christopher Hutsul
Photo of Roger Davies	Charla Jones
Photo of Calypso Arthur	Roger HB Davies

PAWTALK! (PÔ'TÔK) n. Quick, clear, honest and persuasive communications.

– *The Tail-Waggers Dictionary of the English Language*

PRAISE FOR MASTERING COMMUNICATIONS

An extraordinarily useful, hilarious, indeed totally painless way to master clear communication. Roger Davies charms you into his dialogue with his dog, barking you back to the basics of plain talk. A delightfully original approach to personal and business communication."

Dr. Keith Spicer,
Author of Think on Your Feet® and Winging It

"**Mastering Communications** is hot stuff! I loved the dialogue between Calypso and Master. They clearly demonstrate two of the three styles. This device made it easy to become infected with the clever idea in this book about communication strategy. I have already found myself using the strategy in my own work and that's the most you can ever expect to get from a book. If only everyone in the organization had **Mastering Communications**."

Dr. Michael Hewitt-Gleeson, Principal
School of Thinking, Melbourne, Australia
Best-Selling Author of Newsell and Software for the Brain

"Virtually every leader has 'improve communication skills' in their leadership development plan. At last, an innovative, practical tool to LEAP!frog their learning. **Mastering Communications** is a must-have on every executive's bookshelf."

Joan Hill, Learning Consultant and Executive Coach,
CORE Consulting Inc.

Springboard Books Inc.

"Fantastic! **Mastering Communications** is a clever and quick must-read for any professional. Especially useful for those who want to quickly convey a technical message – to any audience, especially to those with a short attention span in today's fast-paced world."

Mark Dagys, CA
Senior Partner, MTA FINANCIAL

"Every sales department needs to get their 'paws' on **Mastering Communications.** This witty and insightful book reinforces the importance of tailoring your communication style to an audience when presenting and positioning solutions. It is the 'must-have' book in every sales representative's library."

Kellie Dennison, former National Sales Training Consultant, Automatic Data Processing (ADP)

"Enlightening. Would help any professional (and family) by throwing light on the communication process, a subject we can't learn enough about. Most failed sales calls, most conflict, etc., come from miscommunication. **Mastering Communications** provides techniques and real-life examples that make better communication easier to apply."

Vlad Bregman, President
Bregman & Bregman, Real Estate

"If you **LIKED** *Who Moved My Cheese?*, you'll **LOVE Mastering Communications**".

Dave McCuaig, Human Resource Director

ACKNOWLEDGEMENTS

When people contribute to a book, they often influence in ways they don't realize: unwitting participants in the creative process.

People like my original business partner, Dr. Eric McLuhan, who introduced me to his father's pioneer media studies.

Like Jacqueline Wonder, who started me thinking about how to apply left- and right-brain research to the field of communication.

Like members of our international network, who motivated me to finally write a book to complement their work in selling and delivering our communication training products.

I also received some pertinent feedback on the manuscript itself. So a special thank-you to Mike Wert, founder and former CEO of DiMark Inc. To Christie Day for being my consultative copy-editor. And to Jacqueline Throop-Robinson, for being my adult-learning specialist.

Thanks also to those who commented on the manuscript: Marc Dagys, John Dames, Kellie Dennison, Ken Everett, Bob Jones, Sharon Lockwood, Des Mackle, Martha Moore, Karen Schuch, Denise Thompson.

And finally a thank-you to the team at McLuhan & Davies without whom this wouldn't have been written.

A WORD ABOUT THE LANGUAGE AND THE LEARNING

As you will see, **Mastering Communications** contains a mix of British, Australian, American, and Tail-Wagger slang.

I've chosen to leave many such words as written where I hope the meaning is clear. In some cases, out of deference to our international audience, I've chosen to footnote the word or phrase.

You will also notice some repetition in the text and in the summaries — inserted to help you absorb the concepts.

Welcome to **Mastering Communications**!

Roger HB Davies

For the two Leapers! in my life ...
Jazz, and Calypso, of course

THE STORY BEHIND MASTERING COMMUNICATIONS

When you think, do you think in words or images?

In a way, this simple question started it all.

It was a question we routinely asked in the early 1980s of participants who took our business-writing workshops. In other words, if I mention the word "boat," can you see the image of a boat, or the actual word?

Words or images? A McLuhanesque question, if I ever heard one. Which of course it was, put forward by my partner at the time, Dr. Eric McLuhan.

McLuhan: *The* name in communications, earned by Eric's father, Dr. Marshall McLuhan, media guru, academic — and probably the world's most famous theorist on communication and media studies.

Many people don't realize the McLuhans were among the first to undertake left- and right-brain research.

The research led to insights that people think in either words or images. Our preference indicated a bias in our thinking: left-brain-dominated people tend to think more in words; right-brained people tend to think more in images.

This bias indicated to us how to successfully approach an audience, and how to approach communication-skills training.

In those early days, our question about words or images produced an audience response of 50/50. Today, we ask the question and few realize it's even possible to think in words at all. For many of us, images are all we can "see."

In fact, much communication has become so visual, so instant, and so non-reflective, it's easy to forget its classical roots.

Those versed in classical rhetoric know communication involves three objectives: to inform, to persuade, to entertain. But how to make this relevant in today's increasingly right-brain world?

The McLuhans' research showed us that the skill of writing demands what we now term a whole-brain approach. We were interested in learning more, and started to apply our right- and left-brain knowledge to the broader field of communications.

What was left-brain communication? What was right-brain communication? These were the initial questions as we profiled audiences during our workshops and focus groups.

We asked questions, and people like you answered. We recorded their observations. The results helped us to "photograph" the communications process, and establish patterns and a model to define the ways we all communicate.

Before we started our research, we thought we could easily document the analytical way of communicating (the **Think!** pattern). So much of how we communicate is clearly analytical or sequential: writing, spelling, the syntax (order) of the language, etc.

Visual communication (**Leap!**) was also fairly easy to define, although not quite as obvious as we first thought.

What did surprise us was that a third distinct style or pattern emerged, just as important. This was the style of what we call **Relate!**, involving the "people" skills in the communications process.

As you will see, it's the style critical to good communications.

Once we had mapped out what turned into a three-part model, we started to apply it ourselves in running a training company, in communicating with clients and staff, in marketing, in hiring. The model made me a more effective manager, salesperson, marketer, entrepreneur.

For years, I used these findings, these insights, without reaching beyond our clients and our immediate circle. However, the feedback and results around me proved rewarding and encouraging.

- Sales staff saw how to communicate more effectively with prospects, how to shift styles to make a sale, not through manipulation, but through good communications.

- Chairpersons realized how they could manage meetings differently, and adapt to styles around the table.

- Our trainers found the concepts helped them in the classroom to communicate with all learning styles.

- Spouses said they better understood their significant other.

- Parents reported insights into their children.

- Business owners used the concepts to manage their staff, to inform clients, and to sell their ideas.

That provided the good news. But we've all seen the "losses" involved in miscommunications, including:

- Lost productivity
- Poor morale
- Lost sales
- Conflict
- Lack of creativity
- High staff turnover

Put more positively, you will find profit in good communications. It is how you project your ideas and yourself to the world. It is how you convey your professional expertise. You can't know enough about the subject.

You may be the technical expert, but until you communicate what you know, that expertise is severely limited.

I therefore believe our findings will help you – whatever your background.

Look upon communications as an athletic pursuit. World-class athletes all possess natural skills. They also hire coaches to refine their talents. Let this book be your coach to help you get the results you want.

Roger HB Davies,
January 2008

Mastering
Communications

10 secrets to fast, clear, persuasive communications

THE CAST

IN ORDER OF APPEARANCE

CALYPSO .... CHIEF TAIL-WAGGER

MASTER .... TAIL-WAGGER'S CHIEF

LULU .... HIS OTHER CHIEF AND BEST PAL

RENÉE .... HIS OTHER BEST PAL

JACK .... FROM TECHNICAL SUPPORT

CORONA .... OUR VP

PEPPER .... OUR HR MANAGER

JANGLES .... FROM SALES & MARKETING

CONTENTS

BEGINNINGS

I'm lying at the top of the stairs, staring down, and looking extremely thoughtful, I think.

It's an illusion really.

I'm not being that thoughtful. I just look like I am.

In truth, I'm simply watching what's going on.

I sit at a great vantage point atop the stairs. Nothing pads past me in this house without my knowing, and I mean nothing!

Master has just shuffled in the front door fresh from a day of work. He's bringing his work home, by way of a change!

He's wrestling with an imposing metal frame and a sausage roll of paper, his flip-chart, he calls it. Although I don't believe there's anything "flip" about it. We're all in trouble. He's brought this home before. He's up to something.

He raises his head to look up at me and check out the action, such as it is.

He sees a wagging tail surface behind a mop of white fur.

He's noting my eyes as they watch him and as they shift.

I'm watching him closely, yes, and wondering what's going on? What's he doing?

Should I scamper down to join him? For a walk? For some play? For a scarf fest[1]?

I'd rather stay put for the moment, flaunting what some say is my wise-old-man look. Or is it just an old soul showing through? So asks Master.

Though I don't know quite what he means by that.

How much have I got right? Got wrong? Master sometimes asks me these questions, and I frankly don't know what he's talking about.

[1] Scarf fest. n. Tail-Wagger slang for chow.

I do know, however, that tail-waggers get a lot right.

We can PAWTALK!, and Master, in his more lucid moments, agrees.

We're clear, concise – and direct.

What you see is what you get.

Master says we don't hide behind agendas. We're upfront.

He says we're "unambiguous," whatever that means.

We never end up with the wrong end of the stick.

We relate well to most people.

Master says TwoLegs[2] might learn from us.

That surprises me. I thought they know everything.☺ I'm joking, of course.

I find PAWTALK! so easy, I can't understand why they face such challenges.

So later that evening, I ask Master, "What's the problem?"

And he starts to explain.

[2] TwoLegs. n. Tail-Wagger slang for mere humans.

PAWTALK! SECRETS

"**P**art of the problem is that people are too fluent," says Master.

"I'm fluent," I protest. "I can talk."

I grant you that only Master (and a few friends) can understand me! Luckily, over the years, we've all learned to naturally adjust styles and reach each other. That's why I'm his personal assistant, I guess.

"Yes, Calypso, I know you can talk," says Master, "but most people equate fluency in talking with being able to communicate well, and ... that's not quite true. We can all talk, but we aren't all experts every time at getting our ideas across."

"You're telling me," I jump in much too quickly.

Master grimaces, almost imperceptibly, but somewhat knowingly, I think.

"The other problem," Master continues, "is that most of us don't realize we use three very distinct styles to communicate."

"Typical," I say. "Trust TwoLegs to make a dog's breakfast out of it."

Master doesn't seem too thrilled with that input either, but he doesn't argue the point.

He reflects for what seems like an age, then concedes, "Communications is certainly more tricky for TwoLegs. But, as long as you are aware of the three styles and know how to use them, you're halfway there."

"Halfway where?" I ask.

Master looks slightly frustrated. "Well, halfway to being an expert ... at getting your ideas across, and getting what you want."

"I'm an expert," I reply, with perhaps too much gusto.

"Yes, I agree whole-heartedly," says Master, "We usually know what you want."

That's reassuring, I am led to believe.

"How come I need to know about these styles?" I persist.

"Because you would understand TwoLegs better," assures Master.

I need all the help I can muster, I'm thinking.

"Also, TwoLegs would understand themselves better," Master continues, "and they would communicate more effectively if they really understood the distinct styles of: THINK! ... LEAP! ... RELATE!"

"I like the sound of Leap!," I say.

"I thought you would," says Master. "But if we all use the three styles, it would help us get what we want both personally and professionally."

He then quickly assembles his flip-chart frame and paper (endangering all in the process) and scrawls the following:

PAWTALK! SECRETS

1. **D**EFINITION: **T**HE SKILL OF SENDING AND RECEIVING MESSAGES
2. **O**BJECTIVES: INFORM, PERSUADE AND ENTERTAIN
3. **T**HREE STYLES: **THINK**! **LEAP**! **RELATE**!
4. **M**ANY PEOPLE PREFER ONE STYLE
5. **C**AN ONE PERSON USE ALL STYLES?
6. **A**LL STYLES ARE VALUED
7. **N**O STYLE IS BETTER THAN THE OTHER (**R**ESPECT ALL STYLES)

I survey these secrets and am both impressed and perplexed. Though I don't want Master to wonder if I'm stupid. Which I'm clearly not. I ask a question to break the silence.

"How does that lot fit together?"

Good question, I think, although perhaps slightly disrespectful. That'll keep the chat going, I suspect, which it does.

"Well, when people communicate," replies Master, "they are always trying to inform or to persuade – and sometimes to entertain."

"Give me entertain anytime," I say.

Master seems not to hear me. He rolls on. "Except normally, most of us try to inform or persuade. It's true that if you communicate in an entertaining way, you're often more effective. But that's not always possible in business."

"You can say that again," I say.

Master ignores the aside.

"Of course, people both send and receive messages, either verbally or in written form."

"It's not all talk?" I find that hard to believe.

"Not at all," says Master. "Much of TwoLegs communication is written."

"I don't write much, so how does that help me?" I say.

"Because it will help you understand those who prefer the written word."

"I have a feeling there's more to it than that?" I venture.

"Actually, yes," says Master. "The point is that when people communicate, they usually try to send and receive messages that are clear, concise and direct. Straight-line communication, from me to you. And you to me. No misunderstandings, message received and understood as sent."

"PAWTALK!," I note smugly.

"Right," says Master.

"That's easy," I say. "So how come TwoLegs mess up?"

That produces a big sigh. A stall tactic, I'm guessing?

"Partly because they don't fully understand the communications process," says Master.

"In addition," Master continues, "TwoLegs often choose the style they prefer. Which may not match the style of who they're talking to."

"So they don't understand you?"

"I'd prefer to say," explains Master, "that they may not understand you as clearly as you might like."

"How do I make myself clearer then?" I ask.

"Let's talk about it in steps," he says. "Step One: Know yourself. Know your best style. You're an expert in this style, and you therefore know the style of person you naturally communicate best with."

What is he saying then? This sounded slightly ominous.

"You're saying I can't communicate with experts in the other styles?" I question.

"Well, you can 'reach' the other styles," says Master, "but you must work at it … because it's not your preference. You need to adapt to their style to be clearer."

Definitely sounds like work, I'm thinking. Even more alarming, I might have to change the way I conduct myself. I'm not so sure I like the drift.

"What style am I good at?" I probe, slightly tentatively, and maybe ever so slightly nervously. What am I digging into here?

"Remember, you can use all three styles," says Master, "but you prefer to … Leap!"

Sounds promising, I'm thinking.

"That's OK, I guess," I tell him. "What does Leap! mean?"

"Can we talk about that later?" says Master.

"Why can't we talk about my best style?" I protest.

"Oh, I will," says Master. "But you will find it easier if I start with the most common style, then you can compare that style with what you prefer. It won't take long. Then we'll profile you."

But first he springs on me a whopping skunk's tail[3].

---

[3] Skunk's Tail. n. Tail-Wagger slang not translatable into one word. Its meaning depends on context. 1. A surprise. 2. A blend of a surprise, and a mental light bulb going off.

SKUNK'S TAIL

"**Y**ou need to know that I personally prefer to Think!," imparts Master. "What do you 'think' that means?"

I know what that means. He wants to talk about himself. That's all I need. Another ego to deal with! I'd prefer to talk about myself, if given a choice, which I'm not, so I decide to humor him.

"We use different styles?" I counter.

"Yes, and ... ?"

"OK. Since I prefer to Leap! and you prefer to Think! ... which is better?"

I need to clear this one up quickly.

"Neither is better; both are valued," says Master.

"That's OK then," I say. "So I prefer to Leap!, and you prefer to Think!, so we're different. Could have told you that ... But you're saying that this difference explains why we don't always tune into each other?"

Master hesitates for a moment, but then he admits, "Exactly."

A smirk distorts his face. I guess he's pleased that I seem to have clued in. Although I reckon he looks far too smug.

Personally, I'm not quite so happy. It seems I've dug up problems I hadn't even dreamt about.

Worse still, it is dawning on me to smarten up. I clearly need to bone up on the Think! style, which Master seems to know something about. He is, after all, my Master, and that merits some respect, I suppose.

So I look over at him, carefully, as if for the first time, studying his every move, and ... Wow! ... Skunk's tail!

He lives on a very different wavelength, a different racetrack, compared to me at least, and he just might be ... well ... plain ... (dare I say it?) ... weird.

Just how weird he is (compared to me) I am about to find out.

THINK!

Master relaxes in his favorite blue chair and I can see he is thinking. He's reflecting, silently, trying to choose the best option, doubtless from a series of many options.

He can see so many options that it almost scares me. This takes time, for apparently nothing is simple, and I mean nothing!

I sometimes ask what I believe is a simple question, and he hesitates. He can clearly see depths to an answer that I cannot fathom. He's sensitive to nuances, and all shades of meaning.

I can see the wheels of his mind turning over, processing this, assessing that, but sometimes saying little.

Or at least not as much as me. ☺

Then he speaks, self-editing, carefully choosing the best word from many words, almost going through a mental spell-check.

It. Drives. Me. Nuts.

"Why can't you move it?" I say.

"Excuse me?" he says, slightly put out.

Master wasn't expecting a full frontal.

"Why don't you respond faster when I ask a question?" I suggest.

"I usually respond quickly," says Master. "But sometimes you ask a tough question that demands real thought."

"True enough," I say, slightly defiantly. "But how about a faster response all the time?"

"That might disrespect the question – and you," he says. "That's why I often say: let me think about it."

Yup. That's his trademark expression.

"I don't understand," I say. "If you ask me a question, I react instantly. Why can't you react the same? When you finally come round to an answer, I've fallen asleep. Yawn, yawn, yawn."

I quickly wish I hadn't added the sound effects. Master looks less than happy.

He also hesitates; I could see that coming.

"What do you mean?" he asks. "Obviously, I prefer to Think! I know it's not your preferred style, and that's OK."

"I'm glad about that," I say.

"But the Think! style is the most common one you'll find in business," says Master. "That's because it's a critical skill, which every organization needs.

"In fact, many organizations rely on Think! experts. You'll find the style dominates in many professions like law, publishing, engineering, the civil service, banking, insurance, accounting, the military, the police, science, and teaching. Also, often in software and computer companies."

"All the places where I wouldn't like to work," I chip in.

"No, maybe not, because you prefer to Leap!

MASTERING   COMMUNICATIONS

"But these organizations need someone like you to complement them.

"Besides, you need to know how Think! works, because it's very different from you, and you meet experts in this style every day. In fact, you live with one: Me."

Yes. No prizes for that one. I had that figured out.

"Writers use Think!?" I say. "Oh wow!"

A bit of enthusiasm never hurts, although I sure lose points for sincerity.

Master declines to award points for anything, and presses onward.

"Think! is one of the styles we're good at," he concedes. "That's usually our clear preference. But many writers excel at all styles."

"I know; you're perfect," I say.

Which I don't believe at all, by the way, any more than Master does, I suspect.

I'm sure he detects the slight windup, but he seems underwhelmed, as usual.

Instead of responding to my attempt at wit, he moves to the flip-chart, and writes the following with his favorite dark blue marker:

THINK!

- **V**ALUES THE WRITTEN WORD
- **P**REFERS ONE-ON-ONE COMMUNICATION
- **L**IKES TIME TO PROCESS COMMUNICATION
- **V**ALUES STRUCTURE, NUMBERS, SEQUENCE AND LOGIC

Master sits down and starts to think.

Pretty typical behavior, I'm thinking. This better be good. Why the delay now?

"Hey, you've got me doing it now: thinking," I say.

"That's good," he says. "You're adapting."

I guess that's OK.

"OK, make it snappy," I say impatiently, but I accept that with Master, much more takes place in his mind than meets the eye. He may be thinking, deeply (at least compared to me), but he usually doesn't miss much.

He's probably wondering how to continue this topic, and present it perfectly, with no mistakes, with complete control.

And I am the captive audience.

We're one-on-one, and I can see that he likes that.

No interruptions.

No one else present to confuse things.

Just me.

I quite like that too.

But what's happening here?

Am I trying out the Think! style? ... (sigh) ... That's a **REAL** scary thought.

"Let me stress that we all use three styles," says Master, "but since I prefer to Think!, this means I usually respond well to the written word. So if you're serious about communicating with me, put the key points in writing, especially if you want me to really think about it."

"I can't talk to you?" I say. I'm horrified, or at least pretend to be. I can play the game.

He's quick to shoot the no-talk idea down.

"I'm very happy for you to talk to me – as long as you're concise, and don't ramble."

What's he saying here? I don't ramble. Well, not much anyway.

"I don't like excessive verbal details," Master continues. "So don't bombard me with details. If I need them, I may take notes – as long as you don't talk too fast. Or I'll ask you to put them in writing."

"Yeah. But don't hold your breath," I growl quietly.

Master ignores the guidance, and pushes on.

"The other thing to note is that certain words – I call them Think! words – resonate with me. I will use them more often.

"Words like: thought, thoughtful, quality, assess, evaluate, priorities, objectives, goals, solutions, proof – and anything that implies sequence.

"Indeed, I usually love to hear about anything that involves logic, or structure, or numbers."

"I use those words," I protest, "Or at least some of them."

"Yes, but I use them more often. You choose other words first."

"I suppose that's true," I concede.

Master perseveres, "You will also often hear me using phrases like: Put it in writing ... Does this make sense? Spell it out ... Based on the numbers ... There are three options ... Resulting in... The first priority.

"I'll also ask questions starting with: Why? Why this? Why that? Can you give me proof? Can you show me the details?

"All of this illustrates the Think! style, and shows that I value time to process the facts and produce the best response.

"And while it's true that I may not talk a mile-a-minute like you …"

A bit of an ankle nip there, I note.

"… it's not always that way," Master says. "If I know the subject well, you'll receive a prompt answer."

"You don't **THINK** about everything?" I query. That's a big relief.

"No, of course not," he says. "Since I'm aware that I prefer to Think!, I often compensate by not over-thinking – because I realize this can bug people. So I don't reflect about everything. If it's a simple topic, you'll receive a prompt response.

"If you're asking me what do I want for dinner, that's not so tricky, so I'll give you a quick answer. But if you ask for my input on a complex issue, then much more thought would, logically be required. That involves time. Fair enough?"

Well, I had to agree … didn't I? Quickly.

"I suppose I need to know more about this style," I say. "So cut to the bone."

"OK," he says waving his hands at me grandly. He looks reluctant, but I know he's keen to tell me.

"The key issue is WHAT to listen for," says Master. "Listen carefully to the words TwoLegs use. Are they Think! words and phrases? How do we present our ideas? Do we use numbers to separate them? Do we seem concerned about results? About details?

"Listen to our speech pattern. Are we talking carefully, and choosing each word with care. Are we economical with words? Do we like words? Do we like reading? Can you hear evidence of thought, of analysis?

"All this points to the Think! pattern at play."

"I like play," I impose.

"That's not what I mean," Master points out.

"Just trying to keep the subject moving," I explain.

Then I try to throw him for a somersault.

MASTERING COMMUNICATIONS

"Anything bad about the style?" I ask. He really can't be perfect. ☺

"Anything I need to know?" I persist.

That sets him back a bit.

"I wouldn't call it bad, but there is a downside to this style ..."

"Which is?" I prompt.

He finally blurts it out.

"Experts in Think! can take too long to make a decision."

As if I didn't know! I am well prepared for my next question.

"Well, how do I deal with that?"

"Bug us. Remind us. That's fine. But don't bamboozle us. Just respect that we might need time to reflect over the bigger issues."

"Fair enough," I say. "Anything else important to you?"

"Yes. Above all, no surprises. Don't spring something on us – without warning."

He gives me a telling look. I reckon we're going to return to that point.

Time to change the dig[4].

"How about talking about me?" I say.

Master spins a double-take. I'm not sure he wants to change topic.

"All right," he says, hesitating slightly. Then he observes, "You CAN use the Think! style … but most of the time you prefer not to. You're an expert in Leap! … Why don't YOU tell me how you like to communicate?"

He puts me on the spot. I thought he was going to tell me; now he's asking me. What's going on here?

He pulls over a clean flip-chart sheet, and looks over intently, clearly expecting me to say something.

Silence. Silence. More silence.

He's waiting, waiting …

And it's boring!

Silence. Drives. Me. Nuts!

OK, he wins. I give in. I must say something. I prompt him to write the following:

---

[4] Change the dig. Tail-Wagger slang for "change the subject."

LEAP!

"Let's chat about your other chief," says Master. "Lulu also prefers to Leap!"

She certainly does. I love her. She's always on the move, always changing. Always trying something new.

Lulu never stops, it seems. Her mind flies – until it crashes.

She talks quickly, too quickly for some, I notice. Others pretend to listen and understand, but I know better. I'm lucky. I can keep up as she jumps from topic to topic. Instant this, instant that. She hurtles into life, speeding from change to change, from new to latest, from fast to fastest.

ILOVEIT!

You want an opinion fast? You'll receive one fast. No hanging around. No getting back to you later. No answering a question with another question.

ILOVEIT!

I know where I stand. I get an immediate opinion, an instant decision. None of this asking-others-for-input. My kind of pal.

"It seems to me that Leap! is a really useful skill," I propose, hopefully.

"Absolutely," says Master. "It's the skill of using the part of your brain that processes ideas fast ... that sees an image ... that receives and delivers an instant message."

I'm feeling pretty good right now, I must admit. I clearly look pleased because Master doesn't stop piling on the strokes.

"Every organization needs this style," he says. "It's a bit of the unconventional, the bending of the rule book. It's free thinking. Really valuable in creative fields, like ad agencies, TV, radio, etc., and anyone involved in sales and marketing."

"So it's good to break rules?" I query.

I'm barking thrilled at that prospect. I'm into anarchy, in case you hadn't realized.

"Well, up to a point," he says. "It's just that rules don't impress you, so you'll likely ignore them anyway. But it's part of a mind-set that often produces a fresh perspective. A creative insight. An intuitive flash."

The profile improves every second, so I let Master continue.

"What's really important is that you shine verbally. So you'll find this style used wherever verbal skills are valued and expected."

"I can see that," I say, quite over the moon with the accolades.

"All right," says Master, "if you want me to communicate with you, what must I do?"

"That's simple," I say. "Just talk to me, in person – and get to the point. Quickly. Don't beat around the bones! Remember, I'm an instant kind of fella."

"I know that," says Master.

I try to ignore the wry smile and rolling eyes that follow. I scratch myself until he's finished, and then continue.

"It's clearly a waste of time to put something in writing. In fact, don't bother. I probably won't read it." This he knows. ☺

"But if you must put something in writing, ensure it's just a summary. Or present everything in bullet points. I'll ask you fast enough if I want more details." (Which is unlikely.)

"You won't find me taking notes. I keep things in my head. I just remember things – or forget them – depending ..."

"Depending on what, Calypso?" Master asks.

"Depending on whether I remember them ..."

Master smiles and raises his eyebrows and rolls his eyes again. He does that a lot with me, I notice. I ignore this overwhelming flash of emotion (for him) and continue.

"And don't expect me to fill out any stupid forms. Give me 'multiple choice,' or forget it!"

I rather suspect Master wasn't planning to proffer any forms for me to fill out any time soon.

"Got it," he says laconically. I don't imagine I've surprised him.

"And if you really want to connect with me," I say, "use words to paint a picture, and to paint a vision.

"You mentioned words that speak to you," I continue.

"Words that speak to me include: Action. Now. Fast. Change. Variety. Flexible. Big Picture.

"Give me Action.

"Give me Challenges.

"Give me Change.

"Give me anything New.

"Tell me about Opportunities.

"Give me chances to let things Evolve."

I'm on a roll.

"The phrases you love?" asks Master with a prompt that I don't need.

"Phrases I love? That's easy," I say. "Get to the point! What is your point? How do you feel?"

I love being asked that. Of course, Master doesn't ask me that too often.

"Show me a bottom line," I continue.

"Ask me: 'What if … ?'

"Time for me is in the present: 'now'! Whatever it is, I want it 'now'!"

"Can I have chow? means 'now'!

"A walk? means 'now'!

"Scratch my tummy? means 'now'!"

"Whoa. Whoa," says Master raising his hands, recoiling in his back-off-Buster[5] pose. "Take it easy."

I was overwhelming him with too many details, I guess. Also, too much 'now'.

I change the dig.

"This instant outlook works to your advantage," I point out. "If you ask me something, I'll react immediately. I won't put it off.

"And I'm a fast talker, fast walker, and get-things-done kind of fella," I continue. "Also, I love multiple colors," I throw in for good measure.

I can see Master is still catching his breath.

"I don't see why color makes your list?" he gasps.

"If you want to connect with me, color attracts my attention. I love color. It's just a high priority. None of this boring blue or black or green stuff."

Master, I'm sure, notes the cheap shot at his color preferences and smiles patiently.

"I got it!" he says.

___

[5] Buster. n. informal form of address for a man.

I then note he's mulling a change in strategy. As it turns out, he is setting me up: if Calypso is so smart, let him deal with this one.

"I hear all the good stuff about Leap!," he says. "Anything bad you care to share?"

Bad? What's he mean bad? Well, I have to think about that one, at least for a moment.

"I wouldn't call it bad," I say, slightly miffed. "But one thing ... we usually don't 'look before we leap.' We just jump in, figuring that whatever happens we can fix it later."

"I think that's a fair comment," says Master, perhaps too graciously.

"Also, some Leapers! like to talk a lot," I say. "They never stop. They talk at you."

Not me of course.

I was hoping to stall on my next point. I finally had to cough it up, "Also, we like to look good."

"Well, none of us like to lose face," says Master, perhaps not wanting to admit this either.

There's another item to confess.

Now I gotta be nimble, gotta be ... quick, but accurate.

"It's not that I feel bad about what I'm about to say."

I'm stalling again (not like me).

"It's just that I ... I blame Lulu, I suppose. She hooked me. First, it was the designer chow bowl. Then the cashmere sweater ... the designer labels on this and that ..."

Master must wonder where this is going.

"I'm now sounding shallow and vacuous," I try to explain, "but I'm not really. I just like ... nice things. Things with class, with 'pedigree,' if I could use that word?"

"That's a good word," nods Master.

"It's just that I'm sensitive to image," I declare. "How I look. How you look."

"And how an organization looks," says Master in support. "I agree ... image is all. It's a cliché, but look at the millions companies spend on the way they present themselves. On their image, their marketing, their brochures, packaging, websites ... and the way we all dress. They all create an image and a brand."

Hey! What's wrong? He's on my side.

"But I'm not quite so image conscious as you," he has to throw in.

No, you certainly aren't, I wanted to say, but think better of it. Master, fortunately, seems to have heard enough because he now wants ME to get to the point. The cheek!

"All right," he says, "How can I spot Leapers! in action?"

It's my turn again. Just give me a chance to chat and I'm off.

"Listen to me talk," I say. "Am I a fast-talking, action-oriented, change-wanting kind of fella? Am I a 'now' fella?"

Then I shoot off on a tangent, and Master doesn't seem too bothered. He seems to expect it.

"Oh yes, I'm good at small talk, a great dinner companion, and really energetic to boot."

Then it hits me again. What am I saying?

If I prefer to Leap! ... as does Lulu ... and he prefers to Think! ... where does that leave us? That's quite a difference ... sort of opposites ... we're not using the same language at all.

"Even though we're different, we can communicate well, most of the time," says Master, as if reading my mind, "and that's thanks to another style you need to know more about first."

Promptly we move back to his flip-chart:

RELATE!

- **V**ALUES RELATIONSHIPS

- **E**NJOYS COMMUNICATION PROCESS

- **P**REFERS GROUP INTERACTION

- **U**SES TIME TO ACHIEVE AGREEMENT, BUY-IN

- **S**EEKS OPINIONS

RELATE!

"Well, I can sort of muster all that," I protest, nodding at Master's chart, nearly stuttering, but not groveling I can assure you. I guess I don't quite believe what I am saying.

"Yes, Calypso, you can Relate!, but not as your first choice," he says. "Some people use this style naturally. Others often forget about trying to use it, yet it's perhaps the most critical skill."

"I thought all styles were equal," I remind him.

"They are equal, but for many people, Relate! is not a skill that comes naturally. Think! and Leap! are natural skills for many. People seem to inherit them. Relate! is often acquired through experience. It comes easily to some, but many of us have to learn the skill."

"Why do I need to?"

"It's a bridge to the other styles," he says. "It's like the English language in that more people speak English as their second language than do as a first.

"Similarly, more people use Relate! as a second language. You're more likely to connect, and bridge to someone who Thinks! or Leaps! if you use Relate! Especially if you aren't sure what style they're good at."

Relate! as a second language. I like that.

"Using Relate! also leads to happier communication outcomes," adds Master, much too smoothly, I think.

"I don't see how," I say. "I see a lot of that style at work, people sitting in circles, going in circles. No one wants to make up their mind. They're asking questions, seeking agreement, holding meetings, attending network functions. Talk, talk, talk, and no decisions ... seems like a big waste of time. Big yawn! Gag me with a bone!"

"That's a touch harsh," says Master. "Remember yesterday, when Lulu and I were talking about you?"

"Oh yes," I reply. "How could I forget? There I was napping, minding my own business, and you were yakking[6] about me as if I wasn't there."

I recall only too well. It started out when Lulu said, "He wants to go for a walk."

"No," said Master. "He wants his chow."

Then they really cut loose.

"No, it's a walk. I can tell," she said.

"He's fine," he said.

"He hasn't gone out for three hours," she said.

"He can wait. He's starving," he said.

"He needs to go out!!" she said.

"No, he doesn't. He's fine," he said.

"He's bursting!" she said.

I finally had to break them apart.

"Halloooo. Remember me? … You could ask me what I'd like. Involve me. I'm not wanting too much."

Whereupon the doting parents glared at me as if their son had dropped in from Pluto.

Master now tries to excuse himself.

---

[6] Yakking. v. From the noun yak. Noisy chatter.

"No, you weren't asking too much," he says. "In fact, it's one of the biggest complaints when communication breaks down, that people weren't involved in the process."

"I like to chip in," I say, perhaps a little too earnestly.

"I understand that," says Master. "We all like to be involved. But there's more to this Relate! skill than just involving others.

"It's about finessing the communication process. Building rapport and relationships. Adding the human touch. Creating dialogue. It's the part of the communication process where you stretch your interpersonal skills, your people skills. It's acknowledging and engaging others. It's about saying thank-you."

"Thank-you," I say, quick to throw in another editorial comment.

"Cute," he says. "Thank-you to you too, but you shouldn't take this skill so lightly."

"Oh, I don't," I assure him, cocking my head left and right and looking intent.

I know better when faced with the famous stare-down, normally reserved for when I've taken over Master's favorite blue chair.

"It's a skill you'll see often used by negotiators, and counselors," he continues, "and by those in customer service, in sales, and by Human Resource departments, by trainers, facilitators and by savvy leaders, the CEO, or line managers – anyone who needs buy-in. Where consensus is important."

"I like consensus," I say.

"Yes. But you usually don't dig it out."

He has a point, even though I do consider consensus a good idea. In theory.

"Picture one of your friends," says Master. "One of your favorite people: Renée. Notice how she operates. What do you notice her doing?"

Renée is certainly one of my favorites. She works in Customer Service. She has a way with people. What is it exactly she does so well?

"Why don't we ask her?" I say.

Good move, I realize. I'm getting the hang of this Relate! style after all. It's not so hard.

Before even I can add another word, Master collars the phone to set up a meeting with Renée.

"We'd like your opinion on a few things," I hear him say. "When could we meet? … And where? … What would work for you?"

It sounds like a big suck-up to me.

Renée doesn't seem too concerned, however, and before you can say hot dog, she agrees to come over the next evening.

* * * * * * * * *

We're more or less facing each other, in a kind of circle sprawled out on futons and on the floor. I guess that's kind of significant, but I'm wondering if we're about to wander in circles, so to speak. However, I like to bask in my open mind ☺, so I'm all ears as Renée talks.

Her voice sounds like a smile. It really does. It's non-threatening. It's inviting. It's neutral.

Renée (like me) listens well, and (unlike me) she doesn't quickly take sides. I like that. In other people at any rate.

"We like to be consulted," says Renée. "We like being asked for our opinion."

"Doesn't everyone?" I suggest.

"That's the point, Calypso" says Master. "It appeals to all of us, but it's often forgotten."

"OK. If this style is so useful," I say, "How can I master it, Master?"

I assume he'll like that play on words. Of course he doesn't say anything.

Renée responds instead. "I know what we do. We ask a lot of questions like: What do you think? How would you like to do this? What do YOU want out of this? How would you like to handle this?

"We prefer words like: Team. Opinion. Choice. Consensus. Agreement. Share. Middle Ground. Resolve.

"I also prefer using the word 'we' to using the word 'I'."

This might be getting too subtle for me.

"You prefer using 'we' to 'I'?" I ask. "Give me a barking break. What's the difference?"

"Don't you feel 'we' is more inclusive?" asks Renée. "'We' involves more than one person, after all," she says. "It shows we've connected."

"Can't argue with that," I say, slightly unconvinced, and still gobsmacked[7] at how one word can make such a difference.

Renée can see I'm astounded. She tries to explain further.

"We also prefer other inclusive words and phrases," she says, "such as: To summarize our discussion ... or as agreed.... These phrases confirm for everyone that we reached consensus."

"All of this relating takes so much time," I sigh.

"It's usually important that we all agree," stresses Renée. "That means decisions can take a little longer, since we're interacting with others, asking questions, seeking opinions, and moving toward consensus."

"That's when I fall asleep," I say.

"But it's important to ask others when you can," butts in Master.

"And if you can't?" I sniff.

"Then you can't," says Master. "In fact, It's a factor in leadership: when to involve people and when not to. Sometimes you must make a decision to move things forward – and not involve anyone."

---

[7] Gobsmacked. v. British slang. Astounded.

"You're saying that not involving people is good?" I'm quick to jump on that prospect. More support for anarchy. ☺

Master promptly out-jumps me.

"I wouldn't phrase it quite like that," he says, all too patiently.

"Usually, it's better to try and achieve some kind of long-term buy-in. But sometimes the issue is such that only the leader can make the decision. Or the leader just has to act fast, and no one else can become involved."

"You're saying that's good PAWTALK!?" I persist.

"No. It might be good leadership," says Master. "Although communications usually improves if you explain later why you couldn't involve them at the time. Ideally using all the styles.

"For example, I'd provide a big picture. I'd provide any consensus and proof that was achieved. And I'd show how it would affect the bottom line. That's much better than telling people this is the way it's going to be."

"So involving people is a nice-to-do?" I say somewhat hopefully.

"Ideally, it's a need-to-do," says Master. "It's a skill that you need to try most of the time if you want effective communications."

*   *   *   *   *   *   *   *   *

"Give me another example of Relating!" I say sometime later after Renée leaves.

"OK," he says, "Suppose I want to persuade you to try some new chow?"

Great! He's been offering the same menu for far too long. Every day, in fact. And he certainly doesn't spend his money on cooking classes.

"How would you feel if I just dole out new chow without asking your opinion?" he asks.

"How I usually feel: not happy," I concede.

"Precisely, and I understand that," says Master. "When you were a whippersnapper, I decided for you. But, if I came to you now asking for your opinion, how would you feel?"

That's a skunk's tail, though I cotton on that Master seeks a more positive response.

"OK. I like that," I say. "At least you've given me a choice.

"What if I don't like the choices?" I say, upping the ante.

Master chews on that one for a moment.

"I guess you starve," he observes somewhat drolly. His idea of humor, I suppose.

"So I'm still not happy?" I say.

"Probably not. But I did offer you a choice … that's better than no choice."

I can't argue with that.

"I don't use Relate! that much," I concede, "But I probably need to."

That clearly presents a major grovel on my part.

"Why don't we take this a stage further," he says. "Let's discuss how you can adapt your style to match someone else's – when you want to."

"I'd rather take a walk!" I say, "if you must know."

That tactic always trumps Master, but, as I find out later, it provides him far too much time to prepare for his next sermon.

You thought I was the only one wearing a collar? ☺

ADAPTING

- **L**EADERS ADAPT
- **L**EADERS SURROUND THEMSELVES WITH ALL STYLES
- **I**F IN DOUBT, **R**ELATE! (**P**RESUME NOTHING.)
- **T**HE PERFECT TEAM: **T**HINK! **R**ELATE! **L**EAP!

ADAPTING

Next day I corner a regrouped Master.

He looks far too pleased with himself, and I'm not sure why.

Until I look at the flip-chart.

What's happening here?

He has penned his words in red, green, purple, orange, and no blue.

Color!

Wow!

ILOVEIT!

Pity I can't read his handwriting.

The words look like a mixture of Cuneiform, Hieroglyphics, and Sanskrit, none of which I'm pretty sure Master knows. Anymore than I do, for that matter, but you get the picture.

Master doesn't seem to clue in that I'm totally lost, glazed eyes to the fore.

He presses on, and walks me through his list.

I pretend I'm reading every word, raptly.

I can read, by the way.

If it's normal handwriting.

I cock my head left and right, right and left, and hope my eyes focus on the right spot, at the right time, and that what I say refers to his artwork.

"Now I know about these styles," I say, "What's in it for me? What's next?"

I wish I hadn't phrased my words quite like that. Master might conclude I'm a bit slow. I just want him talking to cover up that I can't read his penmanship. I guess I'm also trying out the Relate! skill, although I don't quite realize it until I try it.

"That's a good question," he responds.

I feel good about that.

"Clearly, you now know more about yourself and your preferred style," he says.

"Oh yes, I prefer to Leap! and I like that," I gush.

"I thought you would," says Master, clearly pleased with himself. "In fact, you're an expert Leaper!, which makes it easy for you to spot others when they Leap!"

"Oh yes, I can now spot them a short walk away." I probably sound a bit too complacent, a complete know-it-all, and a tad too gushy.

"Then, if you also understand the styles others use," says Master, "you can adapt to their style, and they more likely will understand you."

"You mean I must change styles?"

I can see where this is heading.

"Is that so bad?" asks Master.

"Why can't everyone else change their style to mine?" I suggest.

Judging by the look on his face, this isn't what Master wants to hear.

"They probably don't know what you know," he argues. "In fact, your know-how gives you an advantage."

That sounds all right. I have to admit that if I nail the three styles and other people don't, I really would possess an advantage. But ... I need to adapt ... Prompting the **BIG** question ... Do I really want to adapt? ... ☺

Yet, if I connect with people better, move ideas forward, reach goals by using words in a way that others can hear ... that's not so bad ... umm ...

"Let's take this a stage further," says Master. "You prefer to Leap! How can you adapt to reach someone who prefers to Think!?"

Umm … A trick question? I hesitate. Oops. Master's Think! preference catches up with me.

"For starters, I guess I must slow down," I admit. "That will be tricky, but I should allow others time to reflect, and respect that."

I gag on those last words. I'm not too wild about slowing down. It seems I am the one to be challenged.

"And to reach a Relater!?" prompts Master.

Boy! It's turning into an interrogation.

"That's easy," I retort, doubtless confirming status in my Master's eyes as the resident know-it-all.

I know this answer anyway, fresh from our chat with Renée.

"I'd ask questions, involve them, and ask for their opinion," I say. "And I'd use the word 'we' a lot."

Master probably thinks I'm kidding … but I'm not – this time.

"And if you don't know their preferred style?" Master probes.

I know exactly what I'd do.

"I'll Leap! ... I'll choose what I prefer," I pronounce all too enthusiastically.

I quickly see this isn't the answer Master wants.

"You know better," he says, fake-smiling at me, and nodding.

I guess I'd better wise up fast, so I say, "If in doubt ... I'll ... Relate! OK? Is that better?"

Master seems more pleased with this response, although I'm not entirely convinced he believes me. Can't say I blame him.

"That would likely work," says Master. "You could also use all three styles quickly. As in: ask a question; paint a big picture; and focus on a detail, or some facts.

"Then you can see what people respond to."

"OK, my turn," I say. "You prefer to Think! So how can you connect with a Leaper! How can you deal with me? I'm all over the garden ... or can be."

Quite a confession, I'm thinking. Fortunately, Master doesn't seem too concerned.

"First, I've got to speed up," he says. "I need to be well prepared – and get to the point, fast!"

"Also, I know that I can spring ideas on you, and I'll receive a quick answer."

"YOUGOTIT," I say quickly. "And if it's not the answer you want?" I add.

Master smiles. He's smiling a lot today. I blame the fumes from the colored markers.

"You want me to explain how I communicate with you?" he asks.

"Go for it!" I say.

Master obliges.

"I'll tend to present you a big picture first.

"If it's a major topic, I will then present it in small bites, and introduce pieces one at a time, to assess your reaction. Short, quick questions to test the waters. I jump around, one topic to another, off main topic, back to main topic. I build my case."

"Oh. That's what's happening?" I say.

"Yup," he says. "Because if I ask you too big a question and the reaction is 'No' – that's a total setback. Because it'll be an instant 'No.' Tough to appeal. So I move towards a final 'Yes,' by trying to achieve a lot of little 'Yeses.' "

"Clever," I concede. I can see by the grimace that Master doesn't like this word.

"I wouldn't say *clever*," he says. "I'm just trying to communicate with you – and get what I want – by finding out what you want. And presenting it in the style you prefer.

"My challenge is that I often need to present you with a lot of information fast."

"So get to the point," I chide him.

"I'm well aware I need to get to the point," he says. "This means if I have a lot of information, I need to break it up for you, or provide you a brief verbal summary, with details available in writing if you want them."

"Which I probably won't," I say.

"No. I don't suppose you will," he says. "But the details are there."

Whooppee! I'm thinking.

"How do you connect with a Relater!?" I say.

"That's easier," he says. "I have to ensure they are involved in any discussion. I seek their opinion. I consult. I ask them a lot of questions. I'm really interested in how they would like to handle something.

"And I would tend to talk to them rather than write them.

"Remember, Relaters! are adept at all these styles, so putting something in writing is OK. They know writing is an important skill. So they'll do it. Or they'll learn to."

*   *   *   *   *   *   *   *   *

"What if I meet someone I don't know well," I say. "Can I spot their preferred style?"

"Not always," says Master. "Some people are naturally so skilled at communication, you can't recognize their preferred style.

"Perhaps they don't even have a best style. They've naturally mastered them all. Or they have a preferred style and they know how to shift well. You can't know for sure.

"You're better to assume they use all three styles, and if in doubt, use Relate!"

"What if you can't adapt?" I say. "Or you're so good at one style?"

Or you don't want to change? ☺

"Come on!" goads Master. "Don't you think it's easy to adapt to Relate!? It's easy to ask questions, ask for opinions, involve others."

"I suppose so ..." I concede.

"Many people change their approach anyway," says Master. "Once aware of the three styles, star performers, like you, usually change a lot, when they need to."

He's layering it on today.

"Have leaders mastered these styles?" I query. I'm trying to wind him up here. Master doesn't react, underwhelmed, as usual.

He simply continues, "Not everyone knows about the styles. But good leaders usually know how to adapt – or instinctively surround themself with experts in other styles – to create a complete team."

*   *   *   *   *   *   *   *   *

That prompts my thinking.

So we're a team: Master and Me. That's a surprise treat, a real tail wag.

We're both so different, and yet ... we're real pals and we get each other ... most of the time.

Maybe I'm learning something here.

And if you put us all together, a more complete team.

We comprise: a prefer-to-Think! You know who. ☺

There's Renée, our expert Relater!

And there's me, the obvious prefer-to-Leap! ... plus my fellow Leaper! ... Lulu.

Now, if only I could perform all these skills myself!

Is that another tail wag? Or what?

UPFRONTING

I ponder a key bone to chew with Master. Usually I ambush him. Disturb his ordered world. Anarchy! A full frontal flying leap. Jump all over him. All fours leave the ground. A flurry of fur and a flop. Preferably when he least expects it. Ideally in front of someone else.

I drop in on him at his worst: first thing in the morning, before his obligatory coffee, and when he's dissecting his newspaper. Stick my nose under the newsprint and leap into his lap. I'm not considered a lapdog for nothing.☺ Spill his coffee in the process. **SURPRISE!** ... that's the order for the day.

Works every time ... well, mostly ... In fact, if I'm honest about it, it doesn't really work that well at all. Although it certainly grabs his attention.

Maybe ... just maybe ... I need to re-think this one. Since he prefers to Think!, it just might be smarter to give him some kind of warning. Against my instinct, of course.

Normally, I'd simply say, "This chow sucks!"

I now consider a change in tactics as Master approaches. He can quickly see that I ponder something more weighty than usual.

"What's on your mind, buddy?" he says, encouragingly.

I hate the word 'buddy.' In fact, if he hadn't used that word, I wouldn't now say, "My chow sucks!"

Oops. Not in the strategic plan. I scramble to dig myself out of my hole.

"I didn't quite mean that," I croak. "Not like that, not quite so ... direct."

"Being direct is fine," he says. "But that smells of an ambush, a surprise attack ... don't you think?"

We now touch on TwoLegs' semantics, most of which is usually beyond me.

Master tries to explain, after I ask, "What's the difference?"

"Good communications often comes from setting the stage before we talk," he says, "so I know what the topic will be. If I'm prepared, I'll provide you a better response."

"That's better than an ambush?" I query.

"Definitely. Why show me up? Also, why not allow me time to prepare? It'll work to both our advantages."

"What are you saying?" I probe.

"Merely this: Table the broad topic first, so I've a chance to think about it, and then by all means be as direct as you like, when we talk later.

"And being direct is about being *constructively* upfront," he adds.

I note how he stresses the word "*constructively.*"

"Being upfront – or upfronting – means that you say what you mean," he continues. "And you do, Calypso, you tell people what's on your mind. That's an incredibly valuable skill.

"You're direct. To the point. You're honest in your communications. You're straightforward. People know that, if asked, you will give them straight goods on what you think."

And often if I'm not asked. ☺

"Doesn't everyone do this?" I say.

"Nope," says Master.

"Why not? What a waste of time!"

"Precisely."

"So why isn't everyone upfront?"

"I'll try and explain."

Master moves to the flip-chart:

UPFRONTING GAINS

- **P**EOPLE LOSE MORE BY **NOT** SAYING WHAT'S ON THEIR MIND, THAN BY SAYING IT

- **Y**OU CAN'T COMPLAIN IF YOU DON'T EXPLAIN

- **I**F YOU TABLE IT, PEOPLE CAN DEAL WITH IT

- **E**VERYONE RESPECTS HONEST COMMUNICATION

"Being direct and honest is not a comfortable skill for everyone," says Master.

"Do you mean the word 'skill'?" I wonder.

"There's skill involved," he says. "Certainly there's no skill when people blurt out without thinking."

"Do I blurt?" I know the answer.

"Yes. Sometimes," he says, generously, "but usually you self-edit. You've learned the skill of being direct, while using careful language, with neutral and positive words. That approach to directness is a wonderful skill. You don't spit out everything that's on your mind."

"I used to," I confess.

"When you were a whippersnapper," he acknowledges.

"Yes, you've taught me it is sometimes better to keep my yap[8] shut."

"I didn't know that," says Master.

"What?"

"That you listen to me."

"Well, I listen to you sometimes. Quite often, if you must know."

---

[8] Yap. n. informal term for mouth.

Master continues. "What I like about you is that you're naturally direct. Most people hesitate. They don't want to offend, or the corporate culture doesn't encourage it. People are afraid of the consequences. It's easier to NOT say anything, NOT rock the boat.

"In my experience, people lose more by NOT saying something than by saying what's on their mind. If you table an item, there's a chance someone can deal with it. More importantly – you can't complain, if you don't explain. You can't change something if you don't bring it up."

No banter from me on that score.

"But it is a two-way street," he says. "One party must spit it out. The other party has to make it safe to do so. So, if you're the CEO, or Manager, you need to spread the word that you value upfronting."

"And no whining," I say.

"Precisely," he says. "Make your point, and move on!

"You also need to be gracious enough to accept what you might not like to hear," he adds

"That's a big one, isn't it?" I say.

Being gracious. Not a bad idea, I remind myself.

In any event, I like what I hear. Direct PAWTALK!

What you see is what you get.

That's me!

I got it.

*　　*　　*　　*　　*　　*　　*　　*　　*

"Upfronting is about being direct and honest in your communication," continues Master, "not about being rude ... or ambushing people."

He had to add that.

"It's about being upfront, and not having a hidden agenda. It's about being yourself, being honest, and respectfully putting forward your point of view ..."

"In your face," I interrupt.

"Not in your face. That sounds confrontational. Unfortunately, some people think that if you're direct, it is in their face."

"I jump in people's faces, don't I?"

"That's your personality at work," he explains, "which reinforces your natural directness.

"Unfortunately, many people don't know how to deal with this directness. They take it personally. They think you're being personal. Which you rarely are. 'Blunt,' and 'direct' maybe, 'personal' rarely. There is a big difference between the two, which comes over in the HOW of delivering your direct message."

"I'm just being upfront," I say, "the only way I know how."

"As I said, it's a valued skill," he says.

"So can't everyone be direct?" I say. "What about you? You're not usually direct?"

"I can be direct," he replies much faster than I'm expecting.

"But my directness is not usually impulsive. I first prefer to consider all factors involved, and then choose my time to be direct."

"Not everyone likes our being direct," I say.

"That's certainly true," says Master. "So here are tips on being direct, without offending people."

HOW TO BE UPFRONT WITH THINK! RELATE! LEAP! EXPERTS

	THINK!	RELATE!	LEAP!
Dos	Table broad topic for full discussion later Send brief written summary, giving them time to reflect	Be upfront, but ask for advice Involve them in the discussion	Be upfront Get to the point, FAST!
Don'ts	Ambush or bamboozle	Present done deal	Beat around the bush!

PATTERNING

"You've heard of Pavlov?" asks Master.

"You think I'm a complete idiot?"

"No, of course not," says Master defensively. "It's just a rhetorical question."

Whatever that means, I'm thinking.

"Of course I've heard of barking Pavlov," I say. "We endured this in daycare. We all know the story ... about our comrades and their demented Master who clanged bells every time they ate ...

"So the waggers are now stone deaf and yet supposed to be happy. All they want is a quiet meal. Fat chance!

"Then one day, Master goes totally berserk, flailing the bells for no apparent reason, and there's no chow. Not only are the waggers barking deaf, they're starving.

"He was a regular doofus, if you ask me."

"He was a serious scientist," insists Master, "who established a pattern for the dogs."

"Bet they were pleased!" I say.

"Patterns save time," says Master. "Every time the bells rang the dogs knew it was time to eat."

"Or run for cover," I point out.

"Very funny," he says. "The point is that when the bells rang, your comrades received a lot of information instantly."

"A bit too much information, if you want my input," I say.

"I'm not going to argue," says Master. "But we all receive information like that, too – in patterns. It's how many ideas are communicated in our world.

"Patterns attack your subconscious, and you often don't even realize it. They are probably the most powerful communication device ever. Without a pattern, there's less chance of good communication."

"Is this really something I need to know?" I query.

"It's a big-picture summary on PAWTALK!" Master points out.

"Patterns paint a picture in your mind," he continues, "and your experience allows you to instantly match the picture with that previous situation.

"It's like mental fingerprinting. Your brain records the information, like a fingerprint, and when the print shows up again ... presto: an instant match and instant communication."

Master then flip-charts the following:

PATTERNING GAINS

1. **P**ATTERNS PROGRESS COMMUNICATIONS

2. **C**OMMUNICATION STYLES IMPOSE A PATTERN

3. **S**TRUCTURE BRIDGES BETWEEN STYLES

4. **P**ERSONALITY INTERFERES ...

5. **I**NTELLIGENCE MAY IMPEDE ...

"Do you realize that the three communication styles are patterns?" asks Master.

"OK. I hadn't realized that," I reply.

"Yes, if I say the word 'Think!' ... that should recall a pile of information for you."

Yes, it does, I'm thinking. I'm seeing one picture: Master!

I got it!

When I say Relate!, I picture Renée.

When I say Leap!, I picture Lulu – and me.

"Once you learn to 'read' styles, to know them well," Master proceeds, "they will provide you with an instant profile of how others communicate. Whether it's Think! Relate! or Leap! Once you've processed the background to the patterns, you can instantly picture the pattern."

"I can chew on that," I say.

"Unfortunately, not all patterns promote communication," Master continues. "For example, personality types are also complex patterns. Yet, the same principle of pattern recognition applies. Once you've programmed your mind to read and accept someone's personality, you can instantly read it."

"Have I got personality?" I digress.

"Oh yes." He smiles at that.

"Can't I use my personality to communicate?"

"Yes, of course," Master says. "But regardless of your personality, you still use three styles.

"Personalities often impede the communication process. They distract. They impose such a strong pattern that people often can't see beyond them.

"Listen instead for the communication style being used. It will more effectively and more quickly show how someone is processing information."

*   *   *   *   *   *   *   *   *

I start to think of the personalities in my life.

Meet Basil, the Bassett Hound, who has no personality, I might add.

"You're telling me that Basil," I say, "uses three styles to communicate?"

"Exactly," confirms Master. "Although he probably prefers to Leap!"

"What!" I say, "He's nothing like me ... and let's face it ... he's not exactly the swiftest Whippet on the track."

"The slowest Whippet ... and the fastest ... they all use three styles," says Master.

"It's nothing to do with intelligence?" I probe. "Surely, if you're smart, it's easier to adapt?"

I blurt that out, and quickly regret it. I feel I've committed myself to listening more carefully – and adapting.

Master confirms my worst fears.

"You're absolutely right. If you're smart, it's much easier to adapt styles. But the danger is that the more intelligent you are, the less likely you communicate well."

"How come?" I'm confused.

"Because you use your intelligence to defend and use what you're really good at: your preferred style,"[9] Master adds.

"You're winding me up," I say. "You know I'm smart, so I have to try adapting, don't I?"

"I hope you'll try," says Master. "And may I suggest another benefit if you try adapting?"

"Surprise me," I challenge.

---

[9] Adapted from Dr. Michael Hewitt-Gleeson, The School of Thinking, Melbourne, Australia: "The more intelligent you are the less likely you will be able to think. Because you use your intelligence to defend your current view of a situation." *Software for the Brain*. 1988.

"It will help you bridge to all intelligences and all personality types," explains Master.

"For even better PAWTALK!?" I ask.

"For all of us," he says with smirk.

*   *   *   *   *   *   *   *   *

"Adapting your style provides one way to bridge between the styles," Master continues. "There is another way. It's called 'structure'."

"**STRUCTURE!** What's that?"

I can see from Master's expression that I've thrown him a bouncing ball. He answers quickly, however. Hey, maybe even he is learning to speed up!

"You insert a framework into what's being communicated. I'll give you an example," he says. "Picture your neighborhood."

"OK," I say. "That's a pretty big area. Which bit?"

"How about the bit you mark off during walkabout?"

Hmm. I thought he hadn't noticed.

"Oh, that bit," I say somewhat meekly.

"Yes, it's much more precise than the whole neighborhood," he says. "It's your territory. You've clearly defined it, with markers. A framework, a structure that other tail-waggers can spot."

"OK. I can chew that," I say. "But what's that got to do with good PAWTALK!?"

"It's similar to when you deliver a message," says Master. "You must clearly define your ideas. So you mark off your message with a structure – a pattern, to force you to be clear and to get to the point."

"For people who talk too much?" I query. Not like me, of course.

"If you release a mass of words, with no focus," he says, "your audience may not figure out your message."

"What if I speak LOUDER?" I say (my usual solution).

"It doesn't matter. You need a structure so your audience can more readily hear and retain your message.

"It shows you've organized your thoughts. Call it a road map, with markers that focus your audience – and you – on the key points of your message."

"Give me another example?" I ask.

"The most obvious formal example," says Master, "comes when you announce a three-part plan: You tell the audience there are **Three** things you're going to tell them."

That should shorten things, I'm thinking.

"Haven't I heard that before?" I say.

"Probably," says Master. "It's a long-established communication pattern. It resonates instantly. People are more likely to receive and retain your message, because you've simplified it.

"You tell your audience to hang in for only three parts, no more. Not 10 parts, not 20, just three."

"Thank bark for that," I say, "But what if there are 10 parts, or 20?"

"Then maybe your message is too long. You need to break it up. Or maybe you need to present the message another way – in writing, for example?"

Things are about to become more complicated.

"In business writing, structure is handled slightly differently," he says. "You face more options to provide people a roadmap. You can organize writing in more complex patterns, which you 'announce' to a reader by inserting headings."

"Do I need to know this?" I question, "since, as we all know, I'm not big on writing things."

"What you need to know," he says "is that when people read, they skim-read the headings to quickly find out how the topics and ideas are organized.

"No headings means no organization, no structure. In other words: no pattern, and less effective communication."

"We're in trouble then?" I say.

"It's a tougher read," he says, "which you'd correct if a pattern stood out. We all love patterns."

Pavlov has a lot to answer for, I'm thinking.

PERSONALITY PLUS

"Can we talk more about how personality interferes with communications?" I ask.

"Sure. What's bothering you?" says Master.

"Well, I would have thought that using one's personality improves your ability to communicate."

"Let me show you some perspective," he says, as he starts drawing on the flip-chart.

"What can you see?" he asks.

"Circles," I say. "Is this a trick question?"

"How many circles?"

"Uh, three."

"Right. You know the bull's eye? The one in the middle," he challenges.

"The bit you avoid hitting when playing darts?" I say.

Master looks at me sideways.

"Yes. Quite," he says, thrown off stride for a second, but he continues: "Look upon the middle as representing personality, yours and others, and in fact, the way you learn."

"I'm in the middle?" I wonder.

"Effectively, yes," he says. "That's your core."

It didn't look like my core. But then Master is not Edwin Landseer.[10]

---

[10] Edwin Landseer. Famous Victorian animal painter.

"The ring around the core represents the three styles you use to communicate, no matter the personality," he continues.

"And the outside ring?" I ask.

"That represents your message, your content, your know-how."

"I've got that," I say.

"You might face 16 personality types in the center ring," says Master. "But you only need three communication styles to reach everyone – with your message."

"That makes communications somewhat easier," he says.

You know what? I can't argue the point.

TRICKS

I love tricks. My favorite involves encircling Master. He prompts me to sit, then to lie down. I know the routine. So I now just skip a step. Why waste time waiting for the inevitable? I just encircle him and flop. I melt into the ground, legs outstretched, front and back, largely where you'd expect them.

He then teases me with a treat, dropping it in front of me. I can scarf[11] it only when he bestows me with his control-freak nod.

So when Master says, "Time for Tricks," I'm ready to perform.

"That's not the kind of trick I mean," explains Master.

[11] Scarf. v. Slang for eat.

"What do you mean then?" I ask.

"I mean tricks of the trade," he says.

"Oh, you're going to tell me the tricks of your trade, things that you know after all these years in the business, working with this material ... as an expert."

I really pile it on, which of course, Master must notice but seems to lap up anyway.

"What would you recommend?" I say. "Give me the best of ... PAWTALK!"

"OK, the best of PAWTALK!, the tricks," and he writes on the flip-chart – in colored markers! – with words that this time I can read.

THE TOP 10 TRICKS (SECRETS)

1. THINK! RELATE! LEAP!
2. PRESUME NOTHING
3. RESPECT ALL STYLES
4. ALLOW TIME TO REFLECT
5. ASK FOR OPINIONS
6. ACKNOWLEDGE OTHERS
7. TRY ADAPTING
8. LISTEN AND OBSERVE
9. BE YOURSELF (UPFRONT AND HONEST)
10. IS EVERYONE HAPPY?
    (OR DO WE AT LEAST UNDERSTAND
    EACH OTHER?)

"That looks like a lot," I say.

"We've covered most of them," says Master. "It's just a quick recap. It won't take long."

"OK. Move it!" I insist impatiently, as always.

"OK! **Number One: Think! Relate! Leap!** Make sure you understand the three styles."

"I reckon I've nailed them," I say all too enthusiastically.

"Fantastic," says Master. "**Number Two: Presume nothing.** This means that when you meet people, don't presume you can spot their preferred style. Assume they use all three styles, and if in doubt, what will you do?"

"I'll adapt and try to Relate!" I say.

I'm feeling really pleased with myself.

"**Number Three**," says Master. "**Respect all three styles**. All are valuable. Even if someone has a clear preference, that should be respected."

"Even if it's the opposite style to me, right?"

"Especially if it's an opposite."

"Like you?"

"Yep, like me. We both bring different but valuable perspectives to the table."

I like to hear that.

"What's next?" I ask.

"Onward. **Number Four: Allow everyone time to reflect**, if you can. It's always smart to give people time to consider things. The result is usually much more satisfactory."

"Even for me?"

"It forces you to use the Think! pattern. That's not so bad, is it?"

"No, I guess not," I accept.

"**Number Five: Ask for opinions**. Invite people to really contribute. Not for show, but for real involvement. People like being involved. Right?"

"You bet," I answer.

"**Number Six: Acknowledge others.** This is the Relate! style in action: Saying 'thank-you.' Telling people they're doing a great job. Saying 'thank-you' for anything really. It's something we often forget. I don't say thank-you to you often enough, for example."

What! Did I hear that right? Master admitting a failing?

"Can you put this in writing?" I prod.

Master smiles, and leaps ahead.

"**Number Seven: Try adapting.** Observe which style other people use, then try to match it."

"I might need to work at that one," I remind him.

"Yes, you just might," he says, and presses on.

"**Number Eight: Listen and observe.** Why is this?" he asks.

"Because it's the key to adapting," I say.

"Beautiful! **Number Nine: Be yourself (upfront and honest).** That's self-explanatory really."

I especially like that one.

"Lastly, **Number 10:** No matter what, at the end of the communication, ideally **everyone ends up happy.**

"Or at the very least, we ideally understand each other."

"That's a new one," I say. "You slipped that one in when I wasn't looking. And, why ideally? Why not always?"

"It's not always possible," says Master. "But, if you state happiness (or mutual understanding) as a communications objective, it'll often produce better outcomes."

"I'd welcome that," I say. "And above all?"

I like to offer Master the final word.

"Above all, use all three styles," he says.

"For example, sending someone a greeting card provides a perfect combination."

"It's the written word, and evidence of thought (Think!). It's feedback and acknowledgement (Relate!). And it's spontaneous; it appeals to feelings, and it looks good: image (Leap!)."

"A picture is worth ten thousand words," I say.

"Make it one hundred thousand," says Master.

"Make it a trillion!" I say.

APPLI. BARKING! CATION

I do my best thinking, I believe, when I've yanked Master for a walk. After distractions of smell, of the occasional vagrant moggy[12], of other tail-waggers, and the business at hand. So, in between sniffs, scratches, and sneezes … and meeting like-minded souls who are also pulling along their Masters on the night walk, I ponder how to approach my chief.

I reflect on his last stand. His summary. Which all makes sense, I hate to admit.

I have a nagging feeling, however, that I need to ask more questions. Switch to the Relate! style, I suppose. Umm. But I am curious about how I can apply all this further.

[12] Moggy. n. Slang for non-pedigree cat.

Once we're home and settled, I'm ready.

"Master?" I say with a **BIG** question mark in my voice.

"Yes?" he says, slightly distractedly. He's miles away somewhere. Indeed, who knows where? He's wrestling with a newspaper I had ambushed earlier in the week. It's in more pieces than usual.

"Can you give me more examples on how to apply these styles?" I ask.

He looks up finally. "Sure," says Master, and he starts to ponder.

I resist suggesting he get to the point! I'm really being patient. Hey, I'm learning. ☺

"If I'm really interested in getting what I want," he says, "I need to plan my strategy. That's what we're going to discuss at tomorrow's meeting."

Ah yes: Tomorrow's meeting. That should prove a real treat. I just can't wait to hear what **The Others** have to say.

In preparation, Master returns to his flip-chart:

APPLICATION BENEFITS

· **B**ETTER **C**USTOMER **S**ERVICE

· **E**FFECTIVE **M**ANAGING

· **E**FFECTIVE **T**EAM **B**UILDING

· **I**NCREASED **S**ALES

· **M**UTUAL **U**NDERSTANDING

THE MEETING

Pretty motley crew, I think.

There's Jack ... a Jack Russell would you believe? His owner obviously worked overtime on that name.

Jack suffers from attention deficit disorder, among other things. He's in technical support. How he manages to hold the job down, I. Do. Not. Know!

He's always fidgeting, scratching, sniffing, jumping up and down, invariably in orbit.

Close by sits Corona, a very black, overly frizzy and very imposing Poodle, with flashy white teeth recently salvaged by her dental hygienist.

She looks and smells Leadership. Confident. All business. No nonsense. Takes no prisoners. Top draw. She's our VP.

She's probably wondering why she's in the same space as Jack.

"Didn't anyone teach you to SIT!!!?" she snaps at Jack.

"Listen flossy-face," he says. "Get off my case!"

Even Jack has noticed her dental hygiene.

Meeting's going well, I'm thinking. And another remark like that and Corona will snag him for breakfast!

Of course, I'm present ... as is Master.

We've all been given our marching orders: Now that we are supposed to know about the three styles, how will we apply them personally and at work?

Master has also asked us to develop some visual aids to illustrate our apparent learning. (If any!) As you gather, I'm pretty skeptical knowing this bunch (knowing Jack, anyway).

Aren't I the lucky one? Master had briefed me one-on-one.

Corona had also been briefed one-on-one, and has for sure read the material on her own. She's a quick study, I know.

Given that I doubt Jack has read a thing in his life, I'm not surprised that Master had briefed him (and the others) verbally. Group session. Bet that was fun!

*   *   *   *   *   *   *   *   *

Master now tries to bring order into court.

"Has everyone read the agenda?" he asks.

Everyone except Jack, I suspect. And probably Jangles, come to think of it.

"Are we going to wait for Jangles?" demands Corona. Which (for her) is a polite way of saying: Let's move it!

Jangles, from sales and marketing, is late, a skill requirement of his profession, I'm led to believe.

But almost on cue, he bounces into the room – all-too-cheerfully.

He is sleek, I reluctantly admit, as if out of a TV commercial: the consummate Golden Retriever, with silken fur, immaculately groomed, and sporting a bright red bandanna around his neck.

"Sorry I'm late," he says nonchalantly. "Did I miss anything?"

He's also far too affable.

"Right on time," says Master generously. "As I was saying, I assume everyone has read the agenda ... So, what will you all do differently now that you know about the three styles? Who wants to start?"

Flawless, I concede, as Master models the Relate! mode.

This produces a mixed show of tail wags, paws and scratches, but Master gives Jack the nod, knowing full well he's about to burst.

JACK ... ON CUSTOMER SERVICE

"OK, Jack," says Master, "Tell us what is your best style?"

"I guess I prefer to Leap!" he says.

As if we didn't know!

"I also like to Think!" he adds.

No one says anything, but I'm confident we're all thinking: Yeah, right!

Jack sniffs at our silence, because he quickly explains, "Much of my work involves computers, and it's all very detailed, with numbers, codes, sequences. Very analytical."

Fair comment, I have to admit.

We all know he's more at home with computers than people, so it isn't a complete surprise when Jack sheepishly admits, "I guess I don't interact with people that well ... I don't use the Relate! style much ... Guess I need to ... After all, I provide customer service. Since I deal with so many other types, I need to recognize that they don't always communicate the way I prefer."

"So what will you do differently?" presses Master.

He clearly is expecting a miracle. But Jack gobsmacks us with his biggest skunk's tail ever.

"I'll more consciously listen to others," he says. "I'll ask what do people want? And how do they want it? Rather than just tell people, and lecture on how something works."

Or doesn't work. ☺

"And I'll be more responsive to those who want to see something in writing, as well as those who want to see things visually and instantly ... Also, I need to slow down a bit."

We won't hold our breath.

"Depending on the customer's preference," says Jack, "I'll adjust. And if I don't know their preference, I'll try all three styles. And, if in doubt, I'll start with Relate!"

We're absolutely stunned.

Jack's really got it!

Tail wags all around.

Jack then wows us with his client-care chart.

CLIENT CARE
ADAPT TO YOUR AUDIENCE

	THINK!	RELATE!	LEAP!
	Explain	Involve	Show
Dos	Respond verbally when needed but provide written follow-up / back-up	Respond! (verbally or in writing)	Respond verbally and fast (Now!)
Don'ts	Bombard with details	Present only one solution	Beat around the bush!
Tips	Provide written support material	Offer choices	Be prepared!

CORONA ... ON MANAGING

You might not like Corona, but you gotta respect her.

For one thing, no matter what, she is usually right. Annoyingly so, I think.

She's been taking everything in, of course, and is ready for full flight.

She launches into Jack.

"You're not really a team player, are you?"

Jack suspects he's in more trouble.

"I have team interests at heart," he protests. "Besides, we all bring different skills to the table, to contribute to a team effort."

"I know that," says Corona. "What I mean is that it's not your first choice to involve people – anymore than me. I'm not really a team player either."

We're stunned again. Even we spot sacrilege at the altar of work; everyone is supposed to be a team player.

"Some people simply aren't team players," she explains. "Surely it's better to recognize this … and accept it. It's not so bad … It's just that I'd rather delegate to my team … as long they're good … otherwise I'd rather do it myself.

"But I'm a good boss," Corona continues, "because I prefer to delegate and leave my team alone to execute."

Terror works every time, I'm thinking.

"I'm good at both Leap! and Think!" Corona says modestly. ☺

"It doesn't make much difference to me. Although I will usually talk something out rather than write it down. I know I don't use the Relate! style much. I need to use this more, but I want to get a job done and I'm impatient to move things forward.

"Sometimes there's simply no time to involve everyone."

This we know. And she certainly gets things done!

"I need to slow down a bit," she concedes, "and recognize that others need time to reflect, and to achieve consensus.... I find that frustrating ... but now I'm aware of how others react ...."

More tail wags.

"I also now understand why some people find me difficult to take ... because I'm so direct ... and many can't handle that directness. I always thought it was my problem: people thinking I'm rude, and I'm not meaning to be. I just want results. I tell people what I think. And what you see is what you get."

A huge tail wag! (From me, at any rate.)

"And if you really want to communicate with me," says Corona. "Get to the point!"

She then produces her "Managing" resolutions:

CORONA'S MANAGING RESOLUTIONS

CORONA'S MANAGING RESOLUTIONS

CORONA'S MANAGING RESOLUTIONS

PEPPER ... ON TEAM-BUILDING

Pepper has been listening intently. She's another serious type, a Border Collie who lives to work.

"I think I use all those styles naturally," she says. "It's not much of a stretch for me."

Bully for you, I'm thinking.

Originally, she trained as an engineer, but sprouted grey fur, to be rewarded with HR and management assignments. I reckon that defines TwoLegs' gratitude.

"I guess I'm best at Relate!," she reflects.

"It wasn't always that way. I'm really good at Think! It's just that over the years, I've learned to Relate!

"But hearing such detail about the three styles makes me realize that many people have a clear preference. So now I need to more consciously shift to their preference rather than just go with the flow."

This sounds pretty good.

"Then I more likely will communicate precisely the first time ... and get what I want," she says.

"If I know someone prefers to Think!, I will give them time to reflect.

"If they prefer to Leap!, I can expect a quick answer, and the word 'now' means NOW!"

Pepper's on a roll ...

"If they prefer to Relate!, I must involve them, ask for their opinion.

"It'll also help me build teams. I can now ensure complementary styles on the same team, to cover all perspectives.

"Also, we can look at a particular role on the team, and examine the communication style needed. Then we can more readily match the person to the position."

Wildly enthusiastic tail wags spring up as Pepper unfolds her "Building Teams" summary:

BUILDING TEAMS

DECIDE ROLE:
THEN MATCH IT TO COMMUNICATION STYLE

ALLOW FOR PREFERENCES
WHEN INTERVIEWING

JANGLES ... ON SALES TECHNIQUE

Jangles is too keen to end the session on a high. With a big splash. Complete with red bandanna perked up for the occasion.

He's on his feet even before Master prompts him.

"OK, Jangles, go for it!"

"Well, I'm a Leaper! first," he says, "then a Relater!"

I'm not sure about that combination myself, but no one challenges him.

Bit of a smooth and fast talker, I note. And he doesn't offer much to dispel that picture with his rapid-fire delivery.

"Morethananything I needtolisten toaclient, to hearwhich style theyare using," he shoots at us.

OK. He has been listening. Just wish he'd slow down a bit.

"I can see now why it's so important to consultwith a client," he rushes on.

And he just can't keep still, pacing around, jumping right, jumping left. This could tire us all out.

"If I hear they prefer to Think!, I'll provide proof, details. I'llgivethem detailed handouts, and brochures, thingstoreadlater.

"If they prefer to Leap!, I'llgettothepoint. I'll give them marketing materials, but I won't expect them toreadthem!

"Also, I'll create dialogue for Relaters! I've always known that dialogue is important. Now I know why it leads to more success.

"I will more likely get the sale."

Jangles is smiling too much, as usual.

"Perhaps, previously, I just talked at someone," he forges on. "One-way PAWTALK! Hence no involvement. No wonder it didn't work that well."

Quite a concession!

"Now, when I deliver a sales presentation, I'll consciously blend Think! Relate! Leap!

"I'll provide facts, numbers, proof: Think!

"I'll involve people in the presentation: Relate!

"I'll get to the point: Leap!"

As if to emphasize his point, he zaps the lights, plunging us into darkness.

Jangles is PowerPoint-dependent, in case you wondered. It's therefore no surprise that he promptly overwhelms us with his multi-colored visuals, rapidly whipping us through one slide to the next, to the next. He flashes us more whistles than a sheepdogs' trial, a dazzling array of fades, transitions, reveals, flying bones, all dissolving into check-boards and misspelled text. (Or so Master tells me later.)

He uses every color available ... a regular fireworks show, with sound-effects thrown in.

Fortunately, the performance ends fast.

Pow! Bang!

We all vanish bleary-eyed into the gloom.

I see Corona's white teeth flashing, and she ain't smiling.

Master moves to open the blinds for more light. He dislodges them. They collapse. We all jump, Jack to a higher plane.

At least we now see what's going on.

"How about communicating without the technology?" prompts Master, trying to keep us focused.

"Oh! OK," says Jangles.

Corona rolls her eyes.

"You want me to sell you something?" Jangles probes, trying to buy more time.

"How about some silence?"

I'm not sure who said that.

"How about selling us designer bones?"

That we can handle, I'm thinking.

"OK," says Jangles. "I'd open by introducing myself, quickly, and asking a question like: What do you expect from a bone?"

No shortage of response to that question.

"How about a free sample?"

"Give me beef; forget chicken!"

"Give me fat-enriched!"

"Quite," says Jangles, assessing the results of his serial take-up. He's probably sorry he asked.

"The point is," he continues, "I need to get to the point, but ideally I'd open discussion with dialogue, with Relate!, since I may not know your preferred style.

"It doesn't matter what I'm selling. I need to ask questions, and to listen better. I need to assess a customer's issues so I can really respond to what's wanted."

"How about an example?" challenges Corona.

"Maybe you've just chewed a bone that made you gag," suggests Jangles. "I need to understand your preferred state, where you want to be.

"My role is to help you get there: offer ideas, offer solutions. Like chemical-free bones, real bones, Greenies[13]."

"And what communication style will you use?" asks Master.

"I need to use them all," Jangles says keenly.

"If I hear someone using Leap!, I must speed up – but not too fast!

"If I hear Think!, I must slow down ... I also must respect people's need to reflect.

"I need to be prepared with a bottom line. I must create dialogue, create a relationship, question, listen – then confirm what's wanted. And learn when to stop barking."

Ah yes, I'm thinking. When to stop! Good point. We can all learn something here.

"If I communicate in my prospect's style," Jangles continues, "I more likely will connect – and sell the bone."

Got to admit, tail wags all around. Even Jack's impressed, as the rest of us catch our breath.

I suspect Corona still pegs Jangles as a yap artist.

You can't please everyone.

[13] Greenies® – Tail-Wagger treats available internationally.

THE PERFECT PRESENTATION
HOW TO INFLUENCE ALL STYLES

	THINK!	RELATE!	LEAP!
In advance	Circulate agenda in writing, well in advance!	Submit brief agenda, inviting input	Meet at short notice is fine
Follow-up	Refine handouts to show details, proof	Include testimonials as evidence of consensus	Design handouts to provide key information fast

Set the stage

Complete the PAWTALK! process

THE PERFECT PRESENTATION

	THINK!	RELATE!	LEAP!
Title	Use factual title – not too flashy	Ask a question	Get to the point

Use your title to grab everyone's attention

THE PERFECT PRESENTATION

First words are critical

	THINK!	RELATE!	LEAP!
Opening	Announce structure, and topic to be covered	Involve audience in the process	Speed up your speech but don't talk too fast!
Middle	Provide evidence of substance	Provide evidence others have been consulted	Provide prestige solution
Close/ End	Respect the time needed to reflect	Invite questions	Expect quick answers

Your main message must contain...

Your call for action must...

THE PERFECT PRESENTATION

	THINK!	RELATE!	LEAP!
Tips	Start and end on time	Involve your audience, with consensus in mind	Keep it moving! Be direct

Present your message to include all styles

"Master?" I query later that evening.

"Calypso, yes?"

"I'm just wondering," I say. "Will some people want to quickly calculate their preferred communications style?"

"Absolutely," says Master. "Many people will just know their preference. Some may wonder. But here's a quick way to roughly assess your profile."

More work, I'm assuming.

"It won't take long," he reassures me. "First, let's review the three styles."

He prompts me to skim the summary on the next page fast.

MASTER'S
SUMMARY CRIB SHEET

THINK!	RELATE!	LEAP!
• Approach one-on-one	• Approach verbally	• Approach verbally
• Allow time to reflect	• Ask questions, create dialogue	• Speed up; talk faster
• Slow down	• Invite opinions, involve	• Get to the point; be direct
• Be concise; don't waffle	• Seek consensus, offer choices	• Be prepared
• Use impact words: logic, proof	• Use impact words: consensus, team	• Paint pictures with words
• Use impact phrases: "What do you think?"	• Use impact phrases: "I'd like your opinion"	• Use impact words: vision, big picture, now!
• Don't bombard with details	• Don't present a "Done Deal"	• Use impact phrases: What if? How do you feel about?
• Don't ambush, or surprise		• Don't present lengthy written material

"Now place the three styles in order of your preference," says Master, somewhat bossily, I think.

"Which style is most like you and which is the least like you?"

So I scratch out this:

LEAP*!*

RELATE*!*

THINK*!*

"OK," says Master. "Now divide ten points among those three styles. But give at least one point to every style."

Of course, I didn't want to do that. Zeros for two of them was the plan.

But I offer the following to keep Master happy:

LEAP*!*   8

RELATE*!*   I

THINK*!*   I

"What do you think, Master?"

"That's you," he says.

"Clearly a Leaper!," I say.

"You bet."

"What about you? What's your profile?"

"How about my showing you what we all did?" he says.

"Including Jack ... and Pepper?"

"Yes, all of us."

And he shows me what we all had done:

Master

Think!	5
Relate!	4
Leap!	1

Calypso

Leap!	8
Relate!	1
Think!	1

Renée

Relate!	4
Leap!	3
Think!	3

Lulu

Leap!	6
Relate!	3
Think!	1

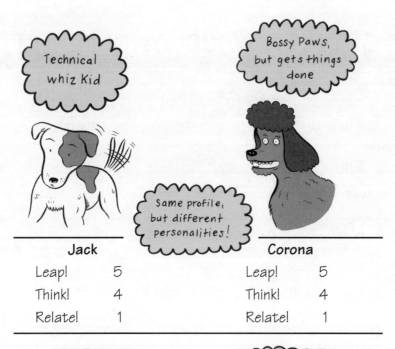

Jack

Leap!	5
Think!	4
Relate!	1

Corona

Leap!	5
Think!	4
Relate!	1

Pepper

Relate!	6
Think!	3
Leap!	1

Jangles

Leap!	4
Relate!	4
Think!	2

COMPLETE YOUR OWN PROFILE [14]

Place the styles in order of your preference.
Then divide 10 points among the three.

THINK! RELATE! LEAP!	
Your Profile	
Your Boss	
Your Best Friend	
Other Key Players in Your Life	

[14] **Assess Your Own Communication Style Online**
How do you really communicate? Which is your best style? What is
your second-best style? To find out, go online to calculate your own
communication-style preferences at www. mdctraining.ca

"Why don't you summarize?" says Master. "Tell me what you've learned?"

"Oh. All right," I say. "How would you like me to present this?"

I'm pretty proud of that response, switching into Relate! mode, as I'm sure you notice. ☺

"Why don't you reflect about it and present tomorrow?" he suggests.

Hmm... I'm raring to go now! Yet, he forces me to Think! I know what's going on.

OK. I will think about it, and come back to him with my best shot.

The next day I really am ready – and I adapt (just a bit ☺) to Master's preferred style:

ENDINGS

I'm sitting at the top of the stairs thinking.

I'm practising my raised-eyebrows trick. I raise one brow, drop it, then raise the other.

At the same time, my eyes shift from right to left, from left to right. Then I repeat the routine.

Cute, I think. It's my party piece.

However, as I practise my routine, I really am thinking. No kidding!

For I now see as perhaps I've never seen before.

I listen. Well, I always listened. It's just that I listen better, and I observe differently, keenly watching TwoLegs' world.

How much have they got right? Got wrong?

I would like to believe I'm seeing a world where TwoLegs use their amazing skills to get what they want.

They say what they want. They're upfront.

They are clear and concise – as well as direct and honest in their communications.

They Think! and reflect, choosing the best options from a series of options.

They Relate! and ask for input, for an opinion, and (where they can) involve others in the process. Where they can be flexible.

They Leap! and instantly respond, when and where they need to.

They use all three skills in concert, for perfect communications. They cover their bases. They play safe. It's communications insurance.

Perfect communications is verbal. It's the written word. It's feedback. It's acknowledgement.

It's the verbal thank-you, followed by the hand-written card, with the colored image on the cover. The hand-written personal note inside.

In words you can read. ☺ I should mention that.

Ideally, TwoLegs listen for cues.

They listen carefully. They observe. They then adapt.

They shift to the style they need.

They're mentally nimble. In their minds, they twist, they turn. They insert structure when they need to. They insert a pattern for their audience.

They change styles effortlessly and you cannot tell which is their best style, where they're the most comfortable.

To them it doesn't matter.

All styles prove equally important, one no better than the other.

Each demanding respect.

Each not depending on personality, or on intelligence.

Each style crafting messages, in a straight-line, from me to you, from you to me.

No misunderstandings.

Straight-line ideas, all clear, concise, direct and honest.

To build relationships, to inform, to persuade and, when needed, to entertain ...

So we can all master communications. ☺

THE **THINK!** SKILL-SET

Thinking
- Needs time to analyze, weighing options
- Thinks shorter term

Listening
- Focuses on content, logic, facts, details

Reading
- Reads text carefully, abstracting the details

Speaking
- Emphasizes facts, details, results
- Delivers structured presentation
- Uses precise, deliberate hand gestures
- Prefers to be well prepared before speaking

Managing
- Manages systematically
- Follows procedures

Writing
- Accepts long sentences, long paragraphs
- Prepares technical summaries
- Notes consistency, inconsistency
- Presents facts logically: outlining, making lists, providing numbers

THE **RELATE!** SKILL-SET

Thinking
- Thinks laterally

Listening
- Listens holistically
- Focuses on style more than content

Reading
- Skim-reads partly for details, partly for speed

Speaking
- Involves audience, seeking consensus
- Emphasizes dialogue
- Seeks opinions
- Responds to energy of the audience

Managing
- Manages intuitively, with flexibility

Writing
- Prefers bullet points, lists, short sentences, short paragraphs
- Writes informally
- Likes summaries

THE **LEAP!** SKILL-SET

Thinking
- Thinks laterally and quickly

Listening
- Absorbs whole concepts, not details
- Focuses on style rather than content
- Reads body language intuitively

Reading
- Skim-reads
- Responds strongly to visual presentation (layout & color)

Speaking
- Emphasizes image, big picture
- Delivers unstructured presentation
- Communicates (with aid of hands)
- Uses analogies, metaphors

Managing
- Manages intuitively

Writing
- Writes informally
- Dislikes (often) putting thoughts on paper
- Prefers bullet points, short sentences, short paragraphs
- Likes summaries
- Highlights visuals, image, prestige

THINK! TRAITS

- Communicates concisely, sometimes with few words
- Can communicate directly, with clear structure
- Sometimes prefers to keep thoughts to themselves
- Provides/prefers written support material

- Dislikes interruptions
- Focuses on details
- Takes notes
- Focuses on results, facts, goals

- Prefers to work alone
- Handles details well
- Prefers detailed meeting agenda
- Prefers time to analyze, solve problems
- Organizes systems
- Establishes and accepts rules
- Focuses attention for long periods
- Needs proof
- Doesn't like to be rushed
- Usually avoids last-minute rushes
- Prefers not to work under pressure

- Doesn't always welcome change
- Dresses professionally, neatly, conservatively
- Stresses durability and value
- May procrastinate

RELATE! TRAITS

- Communicates verbally, wants everyone involved
- Often communicates without clear structure
- Usually prefers to share thoughts
- Needs to establish clear objectives
- Provides/prefers written "image" support material
- Tends to "wing it"

- Welcomes interruptions
- Dislikes details, prefers big picture
- Usually functions without taking notes
- Needs to be involved in setting goals

- Prefers to work in a group, but can work alone
- Can do details well, but not through choice
- Prefers broad-topic meeting agendas
- Prefers to make quick decisions, but can be analytical
- May have an organizing system, although not always apparent
- Prefers to function with guidelines
- Focuses attention for medium to long bursts of activity
- Needs less proof, relies more on intuition
- Tends to leave things to last minute

- Likes change
- Wants to get job done, but can be distracted

- Dresses professionally, but casually
- May procrastinate, to ensure consensus

LEAP! TRAITS

- Communicates verbally, often chatty
- Often communicates without clear structure
- Usually prefers to share thoughts
- Needs to establish clear objectives
- Provides/prefers "image" support material

- Welcomes interruptions
- Dislikes details, prefers big picture
- Usually functions without taking notes
- Needs to be followed up about achieving goals

- Prefers to work in a group
- Does not always handle details well
- Prefers broad-topic meeting agendas
- Prefers to make quick decisions
- Doesn't usually have an organizing system
- Prefers to function without rules
- Focuses attention for short burst of activity

- Needs less proof, relies more on intuition
- Tends to complete tasks at last minute

- Likes change
- Dresses colorfully, sometimes flamboyantly
- Thrives on pressure

- Doesn't like to be supervised
- Wants to be given an objective and then left alone to achieve it
- May need constant feedback
- Appreciates enthusiastic praise/feedback/recognition

USING PATTERNS FOR BETTER COMMUNICATION

THINK!	RELATE!	LEAP!
Think! experts believe they have a job	Relate! experts like everyone involved	Leap! experts believe they have a role
Put key points in writing	Handle key points verbally	Handle key points verbally
Discuss over the phone, or in writing	Discuss and involve	Discuss face-to-face
Supply advance notice	Provide short notice: provide opportunity for input	Provide short notice: values spontaneity
Set goals and follow up systematically	Set goals jointly and tactfully follow up	Set goals and follow up more often
Provide feedback in writing	Provide feedback in writing and verbally	Provide feedback verbally
Provide feedback with logical examples	Provide feedback with people examples	Provide feedback with visual examples
Ask for input in writing	Ask for verbal opinions	Ask for verbal input
Supply proof, provide support material	Supply opportunities for consensus	Supply "experience"
Make creativity part of their job	Accept creativity as part of their operating mode	Make creativity part of their role

USING PATTERNS FOR BETTER COMMUNICATION

THINK!	RELATE!	LEAP!
Supply all details to complete job	Supply opportunities for consensus	Supply whole picture to complete role
Encourage development of systems and standards	Encourage development of consensus	Encourage development of guidelines, quality
Provide private "space" to stay focused	Provide variety	Provide variety and an environment for contact with colleagues
Encourage to work alone, use "Do-not-disturb" signs	Encourage team effort	Encourage group activities
Encourage staff to take time for themselves	Encourage to take time for family	Tolerate staff taking time for themselves
Establish appointment times	Establish both "open doors" and appointment times	Establish "open doors"
Ask analytical questions	Ask for their opinion	Ask general questions
Recognize analytical skills	Recognize team-builder	Recognize decision-maker
Recognize need for privacy	Recognize need for involvement	Recognize need for discussion

USING PATTERNS FOR BETTER COMMUNICATION

THINK!	RELATE!	LEAP!
May need clear specific title	Does not always need a title	May need status title
Expect to receive items in writing	Expect verbal communication	Expect verbal communication
Ask "What do you think about…?" "Does this make sense…?"	Ask "questions." Invite input	Ask "How do you feel about…?"
Direct	Involve	Motivate
Expect some degree of procrastination	Expect some degree of delay in decision-making while others are involved	Expect some degree of "leap before looking"
Reward in writing	Just say "thank you"	Reward in public
Don't rush; allow time to make a decision	Tends to "wing it," so short notice is ok	Will work under pressure; short notice is ok
Expect degree of inflexibility once a decision has been made	Expect flexibility	Expect degree of inflexibility if dealing with emotionally charged issue
Shines one-on-one	Shines as a "consultant"	Shines as an ideas person
Logic	Empathy	Emotion

HOW TO QUICKLY IDENTIFY
PAWTALK! STYLES

	THINK!	**RELATE**!	**LEAP**!
Speed of Speech	Average	Average	Fast
Words that Resonate	Thought Thoughtful Logic Assess Evaluate Think Numbers Proof Structure Priorities Solutions	Opinion We Team Consensus Middle ground Share Achieve Resolve Dialogue Collaboration	Quick Vision New Change Big picture Bottom line Now! Opportunities
Favorite Phrases	The first priority … Let me think about it. Put it in writing. Does this make sense? Based on the numbers …	What do you think? I'd like your opinion. What do you want? As agreed … To summarize … Good point!	How do you feel? Give me the bottom line. Let it evolve. What if … ? Here are the options. Show me the whole picture.

HOW TO QUICKLY IDENTIFY
PAWTALK! STYLES

	THINK!	RELATE!	LEAP!
Likes	Detailed agendas One-on-one communication Time to consider Logic Written word Punctuality Clear objectives	Consultative agendas Being consulted Written and spoken word (usually prefers verbal)	Broad agendas Color Group discussions Quick decisions Spoken word Variety Directness Stories, analogies, metaphors
Dislikes	Being bombarded by verbal details Being rushed Being surprised Being interrupted People who waffle	Done deals Not being respected as equal partner in dialogue	Too many details Beating around the bush Being supervised Long written documents Hidden agendas

MORE ABOUT US

McLuhan & Davies Communications, and Think on Your Feet International are both part of a global network that delivers communications-skills training around the globe.

Our workshops include: Think on Your Feet®; Writing Dynamics™; e-mail Intelligence™; The Skilled Presenter™ and Mastering Communications™ – the workshop that reinforces the concepts in this book.

For more details go to our web sites:
www.mdctraining.ca
www.thinkonyourfeet.com
www.writingdynamics.com

FURTHER INFORMATION

1. *Software for the Brain.* Dr. Michael Hewitt-Gleeson. www.schoolofthinking.org

2. *Whole-Brain Thinking* – Working from both sides of the brain to achieve peak job performance. Jacqueline Wonder & Priscilla Donovan.

Mastering Communications™

To order single or multiple copies of this book,
please go to
www.mdctraining.ca

For those interested in learning more
about our corporate training,
please refer to our websites.

www.mdctraining.ca
www.thinkonyourfeet.com

Assess Your Own Communication Style Online
How do you really communicate?
Which is your best style?
What is your second-best style?
To find out, go online to calculate
your own communication-style preferences at
www. mdctraining.ca

"Of all the workshops I've ever attended, **Mastering Communications** was far and away the most intuitive and useful, both professionally and in my daily life.

"It takes the writer's credo (know your reader) to an even higher level. It helps you discover individual learning patterns, preferences and nuance in order to get your message across clearly and quickly, no matter the audience. This is a skill no one can afford to be without, especially in a hectic world where people don't have time to figure out what you really meant to say or write."

Kim Murray, Writer/Editor

"In **Mastering Communications**, Davies exposes the hidden processes we all use when communicating with others. In a light conversational tone, he enlightens the reader about important differences in communicating styles. As an educator who needs to deal with students, parents and administrators, I find the ideas about communication to be both valuable and practical. The point-form summaries provide a useful reference for professionals who want more from their face-to-face interactions and business relationships."

Steve Murray,
Director of Co-Curricular Activities
Trinity College School

"A wonderful read with impact! And you can use what you learned fast. Provides an important set of practical tools for everyone (from management to sales) to help them interact in the workplace and at home."

Denise Thompson, VP, Learning and Development
ING Canada

PRAISE FOR MASTERING COMMUNICATIONS

"Terrific! Well-honed. A clever, fast, fun read that explores communication from a unique and well-presented perspective. Great resource to help organizations benefit from the differences between us."
Kathleen Redmond, Corporate Coach and Trainer,
Author of Rules of Engagement for Communicating at Work

"Mastering Communications' unique style helps the reader grasp communication concepts that, although seemingly intuitive, are abused and misused by most people most of the time. The chapters lay out the communication styles and then reinforce them with examples and characteristics that suddenly make things obvious! Calypso is to be complimented on his ability to present this information in a way that is so clear and yet doesn't make you feel like an idiot for not understanding it before.

"This book is a must-read for aspiring young people, as well as anyone at any stage of their career."
H. Paul Lewis, former Executive Vice President
Univest National Bank & Trust Co.

"Speaks to the CEO – with memorable, useable and powerful tools on how to adjust your communication style to what people receive best – whether they be team members, customers or the public. **Mastering Communications** also shows how confronting 'truth' results in less beating around the bush, leading to increased productivity and profit."
Roy Verstraete, President & CEO, P. Eng.
Anchor Lamina Inc.